The Revell Story

The Revell Story

Offering Hope and Help to Readers for 150 Years

ANN BYLE

Revell

a division of Baker Publishing Group
Grand Rapids, Michigan

© 2020 by Baker Publishing Group

Published by Revell
a division of Baker Publishing Group
PO Box 6287, Grand Rapids, MI 49516-6287
www.revellbooks.com

Printed in the United States of America

Library of Congress Cataloging-in-Publication Data
Names: Byle, Ann E., author.
Title: The Revell story : offering hope and help to readers for 150 years / Ann Byle.
Description: Grand Rapids, Michigan : Revell, a division of Baker Publishing Group, [2020]
Identifiers: LCCN 2019046474 | ISBN 9780800738013 (paperback)
Subjects: LCSH: Fleming H. Revell Company—History. | Christian literature—Publishing—
    United States—History—19th century. | Christian literature—Publishing—United States—
    History—20th century.
Classification: LCC Z473.F59 B95 2020 | DDC 070.5097309/034—dc23
LC record available at https://lccn.loc.gov/2019046474

20 21 22 23 24 25 26   7 6 5 4 3 2 1

Contents

Welcome

Dwight Baker

From the safe distance of retrospect, it is clear that the year 1992 divided the history of the Baker Book House Company in two. In June of that year, Richard Baker's family publishing business accepted responsibility for the assets of the Fleming H. Revell Company.

At the time, Richard Baker's team lacked experience in trade publishing, and Revell had been badly enervated by serial ownership transitions. Revell assets became affordable—albeit barely—to an independent competitor such as us. Baker Book House Company was prepared—albeit barely—to accept a larger role in our profession. Richard Baker glimpsed the future and jumped at the opportunity, and the rest of us jumped too (or perhaps we hopped). We did not exactly form an executive chorus line, and we stumbled often as Richard conducted the score.

By the time Richard transferred company leadership to me five years later, our financial risks had been diminished. We had learned a few things, mostly the hard way, and new capital was available to invest. The timing was ideal to make the next generation of leaders look sharp, but we wobbled all the same. Revell sales remained flat for seven years as we struggled behind the curtains. Some seasons were awful. New books were ignored. Mistakes were made. People quit.

Yet a core team remained committed to Revell, and it was clear that they woke every day determined to press Revell back into a leading role. Everything became more interesting after 2004 when Revell published *90 Minutes in Heaven* by Don Piper. This success brought resources and capital, and it transformed Richard Baker's future vision into full-speed reality.

In 1992, the historical self-isolation of the Christian book business was drawing to a close just as truckloads of Revell inventory arrived in Grand Rapids. Since then, media conglomerates have acquired or launched six major Christian book imprints. These new publishing companies are smart and well resourced, and they raise the professional standards for all of us.

This is a good development for the church. It means that by one method or another, fine Christian books will continue to reach those who seek them. The hand of God is at work in all this frenetic activity, and his hand is steady. No matter who the participants may be, God unfailingly provides his church with Scripture-based literature. But the value of Revell having an independent owner is singular both for the company and for the church. With experienced leaders who are deeply embedded within our faith communities and with a commitment to its mission, Revell will continue to introduce emerging writers of the next generation as it has done so well for the past 150 years.

Dwight Baker
President/CEO
Baker Publishing Group

CHAPTER 1

The Early Years

Born in 1849 in Chicago, Illinois, Fleming Hewitt Revell was just twenty-one years old when he stepped into the publishing business by starting the Fleming H. Revell Company in 1870. The move into publishing wasn't a huge stretch for the young man.

Fleming H. Revell

The year before, in 1869, he'd taken over printing his famous brother-in-law's *Everybody's Paper*, intended for use in the many Sunday schools around the country. Dwight Lyman Moody, by then a well-known evangelist, had married Revell's sister Emma in 1862. Moody was eager to reach as many people as possible with God's Word and knew just the man to help him.

Revell set up offices in the Arcade Court Building on Chicago's Madison Street, an area then known as Bookseller's Row, at a time when business was booming in the thirty-three-year-old city. The meat industry was going strong, rail lines crisscrossed the city, and steel mills flourished. Industry was fed by the thousands of refugees from the post–Civil War South and immigrants from around the world. These were the days of Philip Danforth Armour, Gustavus Franklin Swift Sr., Cyrus McCormick, and Marshall Field, all businessmen and entrepreneurs who helped build Chicago into the metropolis it came to be.

D. L. Moody

Tragedy struck hard on October 8, 1871. The Great Chicago Fire—its origins are officially unknown, but legend has it that Catherine O'Leary's cow kicked over a lantern in her barn—destroyed more than seventeen thousand structures, including the Arcade Court Building. Revell's business was in ashes.

Not even two years old, the Revell Company faced a turning point, but Fleming Revell wasn't to be beaten. He decided to begin publishing books along with Moody's Sunday school papers, a decision that continues to reverberate 150 years later.

Business Beginnings

The first book to carry the Revell colophon was *'Grace and Truth' Under Twelve Different Aspects* by W. P. Mackay. The book was originally released by a Glasgow publisher, but Revell released an edition for North American readers at Moody's request in 1872. Mackay was a pastor in the English seaport of Hull and wrote a preface to Revell's edition.

Moody, along with knowing Mackay, also knew author and evangelist C. H. Mackintosh, who became known for his premillennialist views. Revell published Mackintosh's *Notes on the Book of Exodus* in 1873. And in keeping with Moody's and others' premillennialist views, Revell published *Jesus Is Coming* by William Blackstone in 1878. Blackstone, a Chicago businessman, helped establish Moody Bible Institute in 1886, first as the Chicago Evangelization Society and later as MBI.

While Revell was busy publishing books, his brother-in-law was traveling the United States and England, preaching to tens of thousands of people and leading many to Christ. Moody's sermons began to appear in collections he hadn't authorized (two were released in 1877), so Moody named Revell his official publisher. Revell never published any books written by Moody because Moody didn't write any. The evangelist preferred to preach.

In 1880, Revell began releasing full-length books of sermons by Moody, including *Twelve Select Sermons* and *Heaven*; the former

Compilations of D. L. Moody's sermons as well as biographies of the evangelist

sold 120,000 in its first year. By 1890, Revell had released thirteen books of Moody's sermons. The next decade saw eleven more, then after Moody's death in 1899 came six more books that bore his name. Revell also published the authorized biography of D. L. Moody written by Moody's son Will.

Another British pastor added to the Revell pantheon was F. B. Meyer, who first visited the United States in 1891. In 1892, Revell began releasing American editions of Meyer's books, including *Christian Living, The Present Tenses of the Blessed Life,* and *The Shepherd Psalm.* By 1903, Revell's list included forty-two titles by Meyer and twenty-nine with Moody's name attached.

Before the turn of the century, Revell's author list included titles by R. A. Torrey, an associate of Moody's; Henry Drummond; C. H. Spurgeon; and Hannah Whitall Smith, as well as novels by Charles Gordon under the pen name Ralph Connor. Revell published religious fiction and missionary biographies as well as books for Sunday school workers, musicians, women, youth, and children. It had offices in Chicago, New York, Toronto, London, and Edinburgh. In less than thirty years, the company started by a man barely out of his teens had become the largest American publisher of religious books.

Reaching a Broader Audience

D. L. Moody had long thought that more people would read quality Christian books if they were less costly. To that end, he and Revell collaborated on the Colportage Library series of mass-market paperbacks that retailed for ten to twenty cents each. Colporteurs—those who peddled books, newspapers, and other materials—sold the books door-to-door across the country and in England to an eager public. In the early years, some sellers rode horseback to peddle their wares.

Hannah Whitall Smith

By the mid-1870s, Hannah Whitall Smith and her husband, Robert Pearsall Smith, had established themselves as popular speakers in the Holiness movement. The pair, both raised as Quakers, had left the Quaker church; Smith was ultimately disowned by her wealthy Philadelphia family, though in later years they relented and welcomed her back. She remained a devotee of the Holiness movement, following her husband to England to preach as part of that country's Higher Life movement, akin to the United States' Holiness tradition. The pair moved back to Philadelphia in 1875 when her husband was implicated in a scandal. At that point she turned to writing.

While she might have been perceived as a peaceful and God-fearing matriarch, Smith's life was anything but serene. Her husband suffered nervous breakdowns and had affairs, ultimately calling himself an agnostic. Though the pair never divorced, they were never able to resolve their issues. Smith also lost four of her children—one at age eighteen to typhoid fever, one at age five to unknown causes, one at age nine to scarlet fever, and one stillborn—and her three living children rejected the Christian faith.

Yet through it all Smith remained steadfast in her faith and her zest for life, never giving in to what could have devastated her. She was hurt, of course, but truly trusted God in all things. She was a strong supporter of women's suffrage and joined forces with Susan B. Anthony and others to give speeches supporting a woman's right to vote. She bought property in the state of Wyoming when it became the first state to grant women the right to vote.

Smith's book *The Christian's Secret of a Happy Life* was published by Revell in 1875. In its first ten years, the book sold thirty-five thousand copies; by 1943 it had sold five hundred thousand. The book was translated into several languages and sold two million copies around the world.

She also wrote *Every-Day Religion, or The Common-Sense Teaching of the Bible* (1893), and *The Unselfishness of God and How I Discovered It: A Spiritual Autobiography* (1903). She helped found the Woman's Christian Temperance Union in 1874. Smith and her husband eventually moved back to England in 1888; she died there in 1911.

In all, around two hundred titles were in the Colportage Library, many by familiar names such as Moody, Mackay, Meyer, Spurgeon, and Torrey. Women such as Mrs. O. F. Walton, Hesba Stretton, Sara C. Palmer, and Anna P. Wright also contributed volumes to the series that included stories for children, short novels, poetry, Moody's sermons, and theological texts. Some books in the series have been reprinted with new covers, and some are available for purchase on Amazon, eBay, and other sites.

The Bible Institute Colportage Association was founded in 1894 with help from Fleming Revell and with the publisher handling trade sales. It became Moody Publishers in 1941.

In the prosperous years before and after the turn of the century, Revell moved into publishing more general-market titles, such as *The Bondage of Ballinger* by Roswell Field, and contemplated an even bigger move.

Revell's 1880 and 1892 contracts with Lafayette H. Bunnell for his books about the discovery of Yosemite

1886 contract with J. L. Barlow for a book entitled *Endless Being*

Revell had long had an office in New York City, considered to be the center of American publishing. The New York office was managed by S. Edgar Briggs and maintained its own editorial, business, and production departments.

Revell's vice president, George H. Doran, advocated both the move into the general market and consolidating offices. Fleming Revell resisted such efforts at first, but he liked the idea of operating more economically, and he wanted to live in New York anyway. Soon the move was made, with the publishing company taking up residence at 158 Fifth Avenue, the Presbyterian Building, where it remained from 1905 to 1950.

CHAPTER 2

The East Coast Years

Revell was an East Coast publisher for eighty-five years. The first forty-five of those were spent on Fifth Avenue before spending some time in Westwood, New Jersey, in two different locations, and twenty-two years in Old Tappan, New Jersey. The final East Coast location was on White Plains Road in Tarrytown, New York.

While the company began to move into general-market publishing, it stayed true to its evangelical roots. Fleming Revell sought to create a balance between popular and more serious Christian books that aimed to deepen a reader's spiritual walk. Two of the authors who helped were S. D. Gordon and Newell Dwight Hillis.

Gordon was a YMCA executive who became a popular speaker in high demand, as well as a prolific author. His first book, *Quiet Talks on Power*, released in 1903 and sold five hundred thousand copies in forty years. Between 1909 and 1915, Revell published fourteen of Gordon's books, most titles beginning with *Quiet Talks*

Books by S. D. Gordon

or *A Quiet Talk*. When Gordon died in 1936, he had more than thirty books to his credit.

Hillis, pastor of First Presbyterian Church in Evanston, Illinois, was encouraged to think about publication by Revell's then vice president George Doran, who attended his church, and Revell himself. Hillis's first book was *A Man's Value to Society: Studies in Self-Culture and Character* (1896). Several subsequent books, based on his numerous lectures, were instrumental in urging the United States to enter World War I. *Studies of the Great War*, *The Blot on the Kaiser's 'Scutcheon*, and *German Atrocities*, all published by Revell, helped sway the masses.

Hillis, who would eventually pastor Plymouth Congregational Church in Brooklyn, New York, for twenty-five years, contributed twenty books to Revell's list.

Another key author during this era was G. Campbell Morgan, who was influenced by D. L. Moody as a young boy and subsequently became an itinerant preacher in England and the United States. Moody and Morgan became acquainted through their preaching, and in 1896 Morgan spoke at Moody's Northfield (Massachusetts) Conference and at his Bible Institute in Chicago. In 1897, Revell published Morgan's *Discipleship*, the first in a long line of his books, marking the start of a relationship that lasted nearly fifty years.

From 1905 to 1931, Revell published twenty-three books by Morgan and, by the time of Morgan's death in 1945, more than fifty in all. Titles included *The Analyzed Bible* (a ten-volume set) and the four-volume *Living Messages of the Books of the Bible*.

Morgan also became a spokesperson for the fundamentalist movement that protested the dominance of modernism in the Protestant denominations, with Revell becoming the publishing platform for the movement's leaders. In all, Revell published twenty-nine titles directly tied to the fundamentalist-modernist controversy, which ran from 1918 to 1929. Authors included Morgan (five books), William Jennings Bryan (six books), Clarence Macartney (five books), William Bell Riley (two books), R. A. Torrey (six books), and James M. Gray (five books).

Books by William Jennings Bryan

Books by James M. Gray

Yet the publishing house didn't restrict itself to authors speaking out of the fundamentalist movement. Revell also published Harry Emerson Fosdick and Robert E. Speer. Revell released Fosdick's *Christianity and Progress* in 1922, the same year he preached his famous sermon, "Shall the Fundamentalists Win?," in New York. Speer was active in the Presbyterian church leadership, with Revell publishing his books before the fundamentalist controversy and throughout the 1920s. His titles with Revell include *Christianity and the Nations* (1910) and *Seeking the Mind of Christ* (1926).

New Leadership

Fleming H. Revell had led his company for fifty-nine years when he stepped down in 1929, offering the presidency of the company to his son, Fleming H. Revell Jr. After just two years, Fleming Jr. stepped down and Revell's nephew William Barbour took over the helm. The son of Junius Barbour—twin brother of Fleming's wife, Josephine—had been sent to live with the Revells as a young boy.

Upon university graduation, Barbour joined the Fleming H. Revell Company as a clerk, then was promoted to manager of the manufacturing department. Eventually, he was promoted to treasurer of the company (and member of the board), and he became the company's president in 1931. Taking over in the midst of the Great Depression, William Barbour led the company for thirty-one years. His son William Barbour Jr. joined Revell's sales staff in 1944 after serving in the US Army Air Force as a pilot. In 1953, after Air Force service during the Korean conflict, William Jr.'s brother, Hugh Revell Barbour, joined the sales force at Revell, retiring in 1981. Hugh's nephew and son of William, Bruce Barbour, became a vice president of sales and marketing for Revell.

Religion publishers had weathered the depression of 1893 pretty well, but the Great Depression was a bit rougher. It wasn't until 1936 that book production in general saw an increase, and Revell's output that year was the highest of all religion publishers.

The popularity of Vance Havner, who was discovered by Revell during the early 1930s, likely helped the publisher regain ground. Havner's first book, *By the Still Waters*, released in 1934, and by 1940 he had four books with the company. A former pastor, Havner traveled the world speaking almost until his death in 1986, by which time Revell had published more than thirty of his books.

Hugh R. Barbour (left) and William Barbour (right) in 1976

The 1940s were tumultuous as World War II raged. Even so, Revell continued its ascent as a publisher of Christian books. An arrangement was reached with the YMCA and its publishing arm, Association Press, to jointly publish under its and Revell's imprints, with books promoted and sold like other Revell titles. Revell purchased Appleton's hymnbook department in 1945 and also became the exclusive distributor of Pickering and Inglis (1947–59) and InterVarsity (1948–54).

One of the biggest surprises of that era was the success of *Mr. Jones, Meet the Master*. Catherine Marshall had compiled sermons her husband, the late Reverend Peter Marshall, had preached at New York Avenue Presbyterian Church in Washington, DC, along with prayers he'd offered as Senate chaplain. Revell published the book in 1949.

This book of sermons, written in language the common reader understood, took off, selling well in religious and general-market bookstores. "We asked ourselves, 'Why did this happen—and how can we make it happen again?'" William Barbour Jr. said in a later interview. Before 1949, Revell "served primarily ministers, Sunday school teachers, and active church laymen." As the success of *Mr. Jones* mounted, Revell "started keying in on the layman more than on the religious worker. . . . In trying to meet the rising interest of the layperson in spiritual matters, we found that other laypeople could possibly reach them more effectively."

Revell's interest in trade books was born. Instead of publishing only theological books for pastors, professors, and church leaders, Revell began targeting the people sitting in the pews every Sunday. One of the most profitable sales outlets was department store bookstores, according to Hugh Barbour, who covered Revell sales on the West Coast and then in fifteen states on the East Coast before moving into marketing and production.

"Our biggest markets were Christian bookstores and department store bookstores, which in those days were located on the main floor and sold a lot of books," said Hugh Barbour, now ninety. "I remember going to Gimbels, Macy's, Kaufmann's, and Rich's department stores."

New Emphasis

One of the first books marking this new emphasis was *God's Psychiatry* by Charles L. Allen, published in 1953. In its first twenty-five years, it sold nearly a million copies, many of those through general-market stores. The year 1953 also saw the release of Dale Evans Rogers's *Angel Unaware*, which, by 1977, had sold more than a million copies.

Rogers, movie-star wife of Roy Rogers, wrote the book to describe the blessings she and her husband received from their daughter, Robin Elizabeth, who was born with Down syndrome and died just before her second birthday. Rogers went on to write fourteen additional books with Revell.

In 1963, during the six-year tenure of Wilbur Davies as Revell's president, Spire Books was launched. The line of religious mass-market paperbacks was the modern version of Moody's Colportage Library and appealed

to the same readers eager for excellent content at reasonable prices. Almost 75 percent of Spire Books came from Revell's list—trade books reprinted in mass-market paperback size—and were sold in religious and general-market bookstores, on racks in airports and grocery stores, and in restaurants and other businesses.

Spire reprinted titles such as David Wilkerson's *The Cross and the Switchblade,* Corrie ten Boom's *The Hiding Place,* and Charles Colson's *Born Again* in mass-market size, all originally published by Baker imprint Chosen Books. Today, Spire continues to reprint Revell trade titles—as well as books published by other divisions of Baker Publishing Group—and sell them in specialty outlets.

Davies was hired at Revell in 1942, and during his tenure—first as sales manager, then as president—he became friends with Herman Baker. Baker, who opened his bookstore in Grand Rapids in 1939 and began publishing books in the 1940s, often reprinted older, classic religious titles, including many originally published by Revell. The pair worked together nicely, with Baker asking Davies for advice regarding his fledgling publishing house. They could hardly have known that the futures of their companies would become inseparable years later.

Marabel Morgan

Nobody could have predicted, least of all Marabel Morgan herself, that her ideas about marriage—scribbled on scrap paper as she went about her days as a housewife in Miami—would become a cultural phenomenon in the 1970s.

"I had written what I thought was a book," said Morgan, now eighty-two. "A Revell worker had come to Miami to talk to my friend Anita Bryant, who was writing books. I gave my manuscript to him. He said he put his feet up on his desk, read it, and said he wanted to publish it. He said it would be a big book for Revell and that they would print five hundred copies. My husband and I were so shell-shocked and sure Revell would take a loss that we bought three hundred of those.

"It was so miraculous, but it was what God wanted at that time," said Morgan. "Never in a thousand years did I think it would sell. I thought after I'd written it that I would mimeograph it and pass it out on street corners."

The Total Woman helped improve marriages everywhere. "Women would write to me from all over the world; we had baskets of letters, thousands and thousands. Women would send me their ideas and I'd use them. We were having a high old time!" she said. "One thing I realized is that women are the same everywhere. The sentence was always the same: 'Can you help me? Because my husband and I aren't getting along.'"

Her ideas about sex, marriage, and God struck a chord with Christian women eager to jump-start their marriages and with the secular media. Morgan appeared on all the major daytime and nighttime talk shows, and she graced the cover of *Time* magazine, though her cover date was usurped by Ugandan despot Idi Amin, so Morgan appeared on the cover several weeks later.

The Total Woman urged women to "let your husband be your master" and said that "A *Total Woman* caters to her man's special quirks, whether it be in salads, sex or sports," as was quoted in a *Time* magazine article. According to Morgan, the *Time* editor mentioned at a cocktail party that he was thinking of putting *The Total Woman* on the cover.

"He said he got such a reaction that he had high-heel marks on his chest. He decided to do it," recalled Morgan.

She took a fair amount of criticism from those in the feminist movement. This is what she said in a 1995 interview with Revell:

"To be honest, I was knee-deep in the diaper pail, and I didn't even know [the women's movement] was going on! At one point I was supposed to debate Betty Friedan at Harvard, but she canceled. I was so relieved. It was silly to pit me against these feminists because really it was like talking about apples and oranges. I didn't have a problem with what they were saying; I was just saying if you have a husband, here's how to make him happy."

The Total Woman has sold more than ten million copies in all editions and was the bestselling nonfiction book in 1974. Morgan also wrote *Total Joy*, *The Electric Woman*, and *The Total Woman Cookbook*.

Did Marabel Morgan ever wrap herself in Saran Wrap? Of course! "But I waited until Saran Wrap came in pink and green because they were more flattering colors. Charlie is a straightlaced, stuffy type; he never knew what would happen when he opened the door."

Upon Davies's retirement in 1968, William Barbour Jr. took over the helm of Revell, which also moved its headquarters to Old Tappan, New Jersey, where it stayed for twenty-two years.

"Our whole marketing scheme was to sell evangelical Christian books in secular markets, and we did a darn good job of it," said Hugh Barbour. "My brother played an important role in the success of Revell."

The company continued to grow its list with top sellers written by familiar names: *Mine Eyes Have Seen the Glory* by Anita Bryant (1970); *The Total Woman* by Marabel Morgan (1973); *Believe!* by Richard DeVos (1975); *The Terminal Generation* by Hal Lindsey (1976); and *Hide or Seek* by James Dobson (1974). Among other important authors published by Revell in the 1970s were Elisabeth Elliot (*Through Gates of Splendor,* Spire edition) and Edith and Francis Schaeffer (*What Is a Family?* and *How Should We Then Live?*, respectively).

Hugh Barbour remembers selling *The Total Woman* and *The Total Woman Cookbook*: "That book opened a lot of doors for Revell salesmen, but I heard a lot of jokes and got tongue-in-cheek comments from the department store buyers," he said. "I sold a lot of them, but the women buyers didn't like the book. Christian bookstores were thrilled though."

One of Revell's best- and longest-selling authors got her start with the company during the 1970s. Helen Steiner Rice wrote inspirational greeting cards, but her fame began when Aladdin, a regular on *The Lawrence Welk Show* from 1955 to 1967, read Rice's work

Helen Steiner Rice

on the show. Her first book was published by Doubleday in 1967, but she later chose Revell as her publisher.

Her first Revell title, *Heart Gifts,* was followed by *Lovingly* two years later. By the late 1970s, Revell had published nine of her books and had sold more than a million copies, the majority in general-market bookstores. By the 1990s, Revell, working with the Helen Steiner Rice Foundation, continued to sell new books by Rice and had published forty of her titles with more than 5.5 million in sales. Her books continue to sell today.

CHAPTER 3

The Transitional Years

Revell had established itself as a powerhouse of religion publishing at a time when evangelicals were recognized as a sizable market share and large Christian publishers were growing faster than secular houses. The general market took notice.

Scott, Foresman and Company, a textbook publisher, decided to move into trade publishing in the late 1970s, first purchasing William Morrow, a general-market publisher, and then Revell in 1978, though the reasons Revell was up for sale remain murky. That same year, William Barbour Jr. stepped down as president, making room for a number of presidents who stepped in as ownership changed. Hugh Barbour stayed with Revell until 1981 before starting Barbour Publishing.

Revell, now affiliated with an education publisher, began publishing textbooks and reference books, with the textbook program focused on Christian schools and Bible colleges. Before Revell could become established in this niche, Scott, Foresman lost interest in trade publishing and sold Morrow and Revell in 1983. The next buyer was one of Revell's chief competitors, the Zondervan Corporation. Zondervan, after going public in 1976 and reaping the financial benefits of the New International Version (NIV) Bible, acquired several houses, including Chosen in 1982 and Revell a year later.

Shortly thereafter, Zondervan suffered a series of financial setbacks and was forced to offer itself for sale in 1986. Just before doing so, it sold off Chosen and Revell to Guideposts Associates, Revell's third owner in eight years. Guideposts, a nonprofit company founded by Norman Vincent Peale, sold books through direct-response programs and decided that owning a book-publishing company would be a good idea.

Guideposts Associates, publisher of *Guideposts* magazine, created two more imprints to complement Revell and Chosen: Triumph Books, publishing books for mainline Protestants and Catholics, and Wynwood Press, for general readers.

Wynwood Press existed just long enough to publish its most famous book: *A Time to Kill* by a small-town lawyer and rookie writer named John Grisham.

John Grisham

John Grisham had no idea what he was doing when he started writing his first novel, *A Time to Kill*, on steno pads during down time between his jobs as a lawyer in Southaven, Mississippi, and a member of the Mississippi state legislature.

"I wrote the book on and off for three years," said Grisham. "I was a busy lawyer in a small town with a lot of clients who didn't pay. If I had some time, I'd sneak out and write. I ended up with thirty of those steno pads."

Grisham would hand off the note-books to his secretary and ask her to type them up; then he'd go into the office on weekends to edit and tinker with the manuscript.

"It was my first effort at creative writing," he said. "By the time it was done, it was over a thousand pages long. I cut a third of it, which took a year of my life."

Grisham began the long process of seeking an agent and publication. He made a list of twenty agents and twenty publishers and began submitting. Rejections came quickly; one of the first was from esteemed Doubleday editor Herman Gollob, who wrote Grisham a nice rejection letter. Doubleday would later publish *The Firm*.

"Then came April 15, 1987. The day started badly by going to my CPA. I thought I was in good shape tax-wise, but I owed a bunch of money," said Grisham. "I limped back to my office and was sitting there depressed when my secretary came running up the stairs. 'There's a phone call from New York!' It was Jay Garon, a literary agent, who said he enjoyed the first three chapters, and could I send him the rest."

Garon began peddling the manuscript around New York and got turned down by all the same folks who had turned down Grisham. Meanwhile, Bill Thompson, a legendary Doubleday editor who had discovered Stephen King in the 1970s, was hired by Wynwood to start a new fiction line. Garon sent Grisham's manuscript to him.

"In April 1988, Jay called with spectacular news. Nobody had heard of Wynwood, but I didn't care," said Grisham. "Renee, my wife, maxed out our credit cards and we took off for New York City to meet with Jay and Bill. I was thirty-three and Renee was twenty-seven; we had two kids. But we had a grand time in New York; we were about to be published!"

The book was a flop. Response was small and Wynwood had little money for publicity. But Grisham bought one thousand of the five-thousand-copy print run and began selling them himself. He contacted his local library and planned a huge book-launch party.

"My plan was to throw a big party and sell a thousand books. It was huge, but when it was over I still had 880 books," he said. "That's when I started visiting libraries around the state and doing book parties, trying to make something happen."

Wynwood decided not to reprint the book, but eighteen months later, Doubleday released *The Firm*. Despite Grisham's begging Wynwood to print more copies of *A Time to Kill*, they didn't; soon, rights were sold to Doubleday, and the rest is publishing history.

Grisham still has four unopened boxes of *A Time to Kill* in his office, plus sixty to seventy copies purchased from people over the years. For a while he bought up every copy he could find in bookstores.

"I've got a stash of them and give them to special people. I gave one to Barbara Bush," he said.

On June 23, 2019, John and Renee Grisham marked the thirtieth anniversary of *A Time to Kill*, which he dedicated to Renee, his first reader.

"We had a glass of champagne and celebrated ourselves," he said.

The 1980s were active years for Revell, despite fluctuating ownership, and saw authors introduced who continue to sell today. Two new women authors came to the front of the list: Florence Littauer, whose *Personality Plus* has sold more than 1.3 million copies in all editions, and Sandra Felton, whose *The Messies Manual* sold more than three hundred thousand.

The mid-1980s saw the release of Dr. Kevin Leman's *The Birth Order Book*, Ed and Gaye Wheat's *Intended for Pleasure*, and Willard F. Harley Jr.'s *His Needs, Her Needs*, all of which remain in print and still sell today. Motivational books by Denis Waitley (*Seeds of Greatness*) and Zig Ziglar (*Secrets of Closing the Sale*) saw broad readership and highlight Revell's reach into the general market.

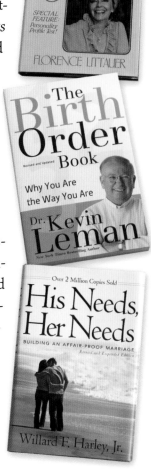

Despite good sales numbers, it wasn't long before Guideposts discovered that a for-profit publishing company wasn't in its best interest and detracted from its core mission. In 1992, just six years after its purchase, Guideposts put Revell and the other imprints on the market.

Richard Baker, Herman Baker's son and president of what was then known as Baker Publishing, brokered the deal between Guideposts and Baker Publishing. His son Dwight, now president of Baker Publishing Group but art director at the time, calls it "a crazy, brilliant deal." Rich paid cash for Revell, Chosen, Triumph, and Wynwood inventory and worked out a five-year payment plan for the company and its remaining assets.

Eventually, Baker sold Triumph to Ligouri, a Catholic publisher, and the Wynwood imprint was phased out, but Chosen continues to be an imprint of Baker Publishing Group. After primarily publishing theological texts and books for the church, Baker Publishing jumped with both feet into the trade book market with the acquisition of Revell and its backlist, and Revell returned to its Midwest roots.

"Wilbur Davies, president of Revell, had mentored my grandfather through his early years as a publisher," said Dwight Baker. "Had Herman lived to see this, he would have been thrilled."

The Baker family: (from left) Dan Baker, Dawn Baker Faasse, Richard Baker, Dave Baker, and Dwight Baker

Elizabeth B. Brown

Elizabeth B. Brown searched for anything that could help her survive the loss of her daughter, a fragile diabetic who died in 1987.

"How do you survive that? I started writing because I didn't find anything; there was nothing out there to tell people what to do," said Brown, now seventy-five. "I eventually wrote three manuscripts in two years because I wasn't sleeping. The first was too emotional; the second for academics. Finally, I put a book together that answered the questions I would have liked answered when my daughter died, and let my friends know how they could have helped me."

Brown searched writers' guides and sent the manuscript to ten publishers. She got calls from a small Baptist house and Focus on the Family, neither of which worked out. The Focus editor suggested she send the book to Revell.

"In less than a week, Bill Petersen called me. He started out with, 'I'm Bill Petersen with Fleming Revell. And who are you?'" Brown recalled. "I said, 'Well, I'm someone who's been there and knows what's needed.' I turned around and asked him who he was."

The manuscript came back in the mail with a note from Petersen saying that the marketing department was afraid of the book because they'd never done a book on the death of a child.

"I called Mr. Petersen and said I could be at the Revell office the next day to talk to marketing, but he said he'd already decided to

go back to marketing and he'd call back in four hours," said Brown. "Those were the longest four hours. He called and said they'd take it."

Sunrise Tomorrow: Coping with a Child's Death released in 1988. Revell thought the print run would last them four years, but reprinting was necessary six months after publication. Brown has written six books, the latest being *Standing Up When Life Falls Down Around You*. She still speaks and travels.

"Everyone has been more than gracious at Revell," said Brown. "They've been so kind."

Willard F. Harley Jr.

Willard F. Harley Jr. has been teaching couples about marriage for a generation. What started as a Sunday school class morphed into lessons on tape shared with marriage counseling clients. Those transcripts of his classes made their way to Revell via sales rep Ernie Richer, who passed them to editor Fritz Ridenour, who agreed a book was possible.

"I would write sections of the book and send them to Fritz," said Harley, now seventy-eight and still teaching on marriage. "He would read the sections, then send me a tape of his thoughts and ideas.

"Ridenour is the one who encouraged an 'edge,'" said Harley. He wanted to make it fun to read, and the subtitle, *Building an Affair-Proof Marriage*, was that edge, according to Harley.

His Needs, Her Needs: Building an Affair-Proof Marriage came out in 1986 and languished for about a year. Harley called and wrote every place he knew to request media appearances before he got on *The Sally Jessy Raphael Show.*

"I was the only man in the entire place: the audience, camera people, everyone was female," Harley recalled. "I was on with two women, one who had written a book saying that every woman should have an affair. The other was saying the same thing.

"I started out by saying that an affair is the worst thing a spouse can go through and likened it to having a heroin addiction," said Harley. "Sally held up *His Needs, Her Needs* and said, 'If I'd read this book fifteen years ago, my life would be very different.'"

The book took off. Revell quickly printed fifteen thousand copies that were soon gone. Another printing of twenty-five thousand sold out as well. Now more than five million copies have been sold in all editions, translations, and revised versions. Harley has written twenty-three books on marriage and relationships, hosts a daily radio talk show, and is director of Marriage Builders (www.marriage builders.com).

"Joyce and I are still working together, counseling together, and running the website. We have a great marriage, which I think is how I got into marriage counseling," he said.

CHAPTER 4

The Trade Publishing Years

William Petersen was one of the few who moved to Grand Rapids, Michigan, with the sale of Revell in 1992. He had been hired as editorial director by Guideposts in 1987, following the tenure of Fritz Ridenour, who had been brought in to help guide the publishing house through the wild market changes of the late '70s and early '80s.

Petersen, who had joined the Revell staff after twenty-eight years with *Eternity* magazine, had been brought on to reestablish Revell in the evangelical marketplace; he referred to himself as a "stabilizing editor." One of his first jobs was to develop a Revell Bible dictionary with Larry Richards as editor and Guideposts as a key supporter.

The Revell Concise Bible Dictionary came out in September 1991 and had sales of over fifty thousand in less than six months. Despite this strong showing, Revell was put on the sales block not long after. Once Revell was settled with Baker Publishing, *The Revell Bible Dictionary*, deluxe color edition, was rereleased in 1994 and continues to sell.

Petersen was glad to remain with Revell. He, along with John Topliff, made the move to Grand Rapids—they were the only two of the company's thirty to forty employees to move west.

"Baker gave stability to our list," said Petersen. "I had to convince authors that Baker could sell books. They could sell theological books, but could they sell more popular books? It took a while, but the authors realized that we could do it."

Petersen, who eventually became editorial director of Revell, encouraged Baker Publishing to put out a little more money for author advances than what they were used to. "This was a tough thing for them," said Petersen. "But they were smart publishers and still are."

Topliff remembers that time well. He moved to Grand Rapids as director of marketing for Revell and was one of the first couple of marketing people at the company. He remembers Guideposts creating Gleneida Publishing for its Fleming H. Revell, Wynwood, and Triumph imprints but focusing on the latter two, which weren't making money.

"Rich Baker had a vision for the Revell program, and he did a smart thing in selling off the nonstrategic divisions," said Topliff. "And he knew how to publish backlist titles. Baker has done amazingly well with Revell, a real testament to its leadership. It's a wonderful fit."

Move into Trade Books

Baker Publishing Group had been what Dwight Baker called a "tepid" trade publisher. Its reach into the Christian general market—

different from the company's usual academic/pastor/church worker readership—was limited, yet Rich Baker saw the need to move in that direction and knew that Revell, with its high-quality backlist, was the ticket. Despite having many owners over nearly a decade, Revell had continued to publish bestselling trade titles. That momentum, however, slowed considerably as Baker learned the finer points of publishing for and selling books to general-market readers.

Five years after its purchase—the time it took to pay off the cost of acquiring it—Revell began to take off. There was capital to pour into acquiring authors, hiring staff, and marketing and publicity. Rich Baker retired and Dwight Baker took over the role as president at the five-year mark.

"Without Revell, we'd been slugging along in trade publishing," said Dwight Baker. "Its purchase was a kick start for us. Our business goal is to be the leading independent trade book company, and Revell set us on the path toward that."

Petersen hired Linda Holland as his successor (he later collaborated on several books for Revell). Holland recognized the talent of Jennifer Leep and brought her into Revell, and she also brought on Lonnie Hull DuPont to acquire for Revell. DuPont had significant experience in the Christian publishing industry, starting at Spring Arbor Distributors, then Guideposts, HarperSanFrancisco, and Thomas Nelson.

"Guideposts bought Revell while I was there," recalled DuPont, explaining that while Revell was still headquartered in Old Tappan, New Jersey, Guideposts provided space for the new Revell imprint called Wynwood in their New York office. "The Wynwood editor, Bill Thompson, used the office one or two days a week. He struck me as the stereotypical New York City acquisitions editor: on the phone all the time, really smart, and making deals. Thompson brought in John Grisham and published *A Time to Kill*."

DuPont also remembers the sale of Revell to Baker: "I remember thinking it seemed an odd acquisition." In the meantime, DuPont and her husband returned to Michigan after years spent in San Francisco. Holland offered her a part-time job with Revell and she took it, eager for stability and a steady paycheck.

"I was an hour late for my first day, but nobody cared because [publisher] Al Fisher had put in his resignation that day. Linda Holland put me in someone's empty office and gave me the slush pile," DuPont recalled. "I was so upset that I said no to everything. For once in my career I was going to work at a stable house, but stability was walking out the door that day. I called my husband to tell him, and he said, 'Can you stay until we get a mortgage?'"

There were no acquisitions meetings in Revell's early years at Baker. Manuscripts were passed from person to person, with all having to sign off. The first book DuPont acquired was *The Color of Grace: Thoughts from a Garden in a Dry Land*, nonfiction by Tonia Triebwasser. Dwight Baker, the newly installed president/former art director, had drawn and colored a coreopsis flower on the manuscript while taking his turn to read it.

"I figured I could work here. By the end of the year Dwight had hired Dave Lewis and Don Stephenson. Fresh blood was afoot," she said. "Things began to change; we started having meetings to make decisions."

Changes included a move from two seasons for book releases to three and, under publisher Don Stephenson, doubling the number of titles overall.

Adding Infrastructure

Acquiring Revell and its backlist was one thing—it was another to warehouse the inventory. Until he retired in 2019, Marv Moll had worked for Baker since its days on Wealthy Street; he remembered receiving cartons of Revell books purchased at ten cents on the dollar.

"We thought it was cool that we were stocking Dale Evans Rogers's books in the used bookstore, then we bought the company!" he said.

The purchase of Revell, Baker's first major acquisition, meant a dramatically increased workload in accounting, order fulfillment, and customer service. The company was forced to expand its warehouse space to accommodate huge increases in new titles and backlist stock. Baker rented temporary warehouse space off-site, which meant shuttles going back and forth with skids of books. The accounts receivable department grew as those customers who had dealt directly with Revell now came to Baker. And the building itself needed more space for more employees.

Baker Publishing Group facility in Ada, Michigan

John F. Westfall

John F. Westfall traded time on his radio show with all attending HarperCollins authors for fifteen minutes with an acquisitions editor at the Christian Booksellers Association trade show. He met with Lonnie Hull DuPont, who was with HarperCollins at the time. This led to a pair of books with HarperCollins and one book, *Building Strong People*, with Baker Books—also via DuPont, after she changed employers.

Westfall began pastoring churches in place of writing until life took a bad turn and he lost his house, his job, and some friends. Friends kept asking him if he was over it, but he realized he'd never get over it, only get through it.

"I tracked down Lonnie and left her a phone message saying, 'I've got a book called *Getting Past What You'll Never Get Over*,'" said Westfall. "That book was part of my healing journey; it sold over a hundred thousand, and I still get emails from people."

Westfall then faced cancer surgery that required him to remain mostly bedridden, until DuPont called out of the blue.

"She said she thought it was time for another book. I told her I was in a bad place but within twenty-four hours had an outline and part of a first chapter," said Westfall. "She offered me a two-book contract, and once again Revell was part of the healing process in my life."

Westfall has been open about his struggles: fear, depression, disappointment. His journey is part of every one of his books, including *Getting Past What You'll Never Get Over* and *I Didn't Sign Up for This: Finding Hope When Everything Is Going Wrong.*

"Revell gave me the freedom to share my struggles; they weren't afraid of that and even embraced it," said Westfall, who is retired but still speaks. "If I can see God for myself, readers can feel like they're eavesdropping on a conversation instead of me telling them what to do. I've appreciated that about Revell; I think Revell has a reputation for books that touch lives in meaningful ways."

"All departments experienced a heavier workload," said Moll. "We had to remodel; we expanded the editorial wing and the warehouse. There was a lot of cramped space, a lot of construction, and a lot of money going out."

Also expanded was the fledgling computer system. Moll was brought to the Ada headquarters to help back up the day's work each evening. The room-sized mainframe had half a dozen terminals at which accounting and billing people worked in shifts (editorial was still using manual and electric typewriters in the early 1990s).

"Often I worked late on the computer backup; my wife would call and I'd pick up the phone and say, 'What's up?' One night I did that and heard only silence. I thought, 'Uh oh,'" recalled Moll.

"Then a voice said, 'Is this Baker Book House? This is Chuck Colson calling.' He wanted to place an order for *Born Again.* There I was talking to this celebrity who had been in the White House and knew President Nixon. He was just a normal guy," said Moll. "It was like talking to a good friend. I took his order, of course."

The days of being a small publisher were over. The move to computers was met with dragging and kicking of feet, but growth also meant seeing authors such as Revell's Willard F. Harley Jr., Pat Williams, and Kevin Leman walking the halls of the Ada office.

CHAPTER 5

The Modern Era

Revell has never shied away from addressing difficult issues. In the early 1990s, titles included *When Addiction Comes to Church* by Melinda Fish and *Gambling: A Bad Bet* by Norman L. Geisler. There was also *The Black Mask: Satanism in America Today* by John Charles Cooper and *Something's Going On Out There* by David Wimbush, a discussion about the possibility of life in outer space.

Authors included Charles Allen (*God's Psychiatry*), Leonard LeSourd (*Strong Men, Weak Men*), Robert Schuller (*What Happens to Good People When Bad Things Happen*), John Stott (*Decisive Issues Facing Christians Today*), and Jean Lush (*Women and Stress*). A Gleneida Publishing Group catalog of backlist titles, put out for fall/winter 1992–93, included Wynwood Press, Triumph Books, and Fleming H. Revell. Wynwood's list included *A Time to Kill*, and Triumph included Henri J. M. Nouwen's *Thomas Merton: Contemplative Critic* and the prescient *Shattered Vows: Priests Who Leave* by David Rice.

Revell's backlist included titles by the popular Willard F. Harley Jr., Dale Evans Rogers, Sandra Felton, and Norman Vincent

Peale, as well as titles like *The Good Book Cookbook* and *A Child's First Book of Prayers*. The Backlist Book Catalog, likely published while the sale to Baker Publishing was in the works, listed nearly 350 Revell titles. All of that backlist, which is what drew Richard Baker to the house, was transferred to Baker. By the spring of 1993, the Revell catalog listed Ada, Michigan, as its address.

In its first full year as an imprint of Baker Publishing, Revell continued on a well-walked path with longtime authors. *A Book of Comfort*, a compilation of verse by Helen Steiner Rice, released, as did a biography titled *Helen Steiner Rice: Ambassador of Sunshine* by Ronald Pollitt and Virginia Wiltse. There was also a new series combining Rice's verse with Precious Moments illustrations by Sam Butcher.

The Thorn of Sexual Abuse: The Gripping Story of a Family's Courage and One Man's Struggle by Beth Sterling, *Silent Hunger: A Biblical Approach to Overcoming Compulsive Eating and Overweight* by Judy and Arthur Halliday, and *Haunted Memories: Healing the Pain of Childhood Abuse* by Perry L. Draper highlight Revell's ability and desire to share stories that don't shy away from life's difficulties.

Women's issues were at the forefront as well, perhaps due to Revell's strong female leadership that knew its audience and also Baker Publishing's fearlessness in looking at the issues of the day. Titles in the mid-1990s included *The Dual-Earner Marriage: The Elaborate Balancing Act* by Jack and Judy Balswick, *Stress and the Woman's Body* by W. David Hager, MD, and Linda Carruth Hager, and *Coming Home to Raise Your Children: A Survival Guide for Moms* by Christine Moriarty Field.

The late 1990s offered a blend of new and renewed titles. One of the first books addressing young people and the internet appeared with *Kids Online: Protecting Your Children in Cyberspace* by Donna Rice Hughes (1998), and Revell addressed pressing cultural issues from a Christian worldview in *Human Cloning: Playing God or Scientific Progress?* by Lane P. Lester, PhD, and *Same-Sex Partnerships? A Christian Perspective* by John Stott.

A third and fourth title were added to the Corrie ten Boom Library, which eventually totaled seven books, many previously published by Revell. Kevin Leman's *The New Birth Order Book*, expanded and updated, came out in 1998, and *Sex Begins in the Kitchen: Because Love Is an All-Day Affair* released in 1999.

The new millennium saw the introduction of several authors who became Revell mainstays for years, including humorists Martha Bolton, Karen Scalf Linamen, and Laura Jensen Walker, and money expert Mary Hunt (*Debt-Proof Your Marriage*). Women were the target audience for books such as *Becoming a Woman of Passion* by Carole Gift Page and *Unveiling Depression in Women: A Practical Guide to Understanding and Overcoming Depression* by Archibald Hart and Catherine Hart Weber.

Revell published numerous books by Helen Steiner Rice.

Women's felt needs were addressed in books such as *Homespun Gifts from the Heart* by Karen Ehman, Kelly Hovermale, and Trish Smith; *Dress like a Million Bucks without Spending It!* by Jo Ann Janssen and Gwen Ellis; and *Scale Down: A Realistic Guide to Balancing Body, Soul, and Spirit* by Danna Demetre.

Other titles in those years included *Ahead of the Game: The Pat Williams Story* and Williams's *Mr. Littlejohn's Secrets to a Lifetime of Success*, as well as *Guerrilla Hostage: 810 Days in Captivity; The Dramatic Story of Ray Rising's Ordeal in the Colombian Jungle* by Denise Marie Siino.

Moving into Fiction

Revell has been a nonfiction powerhouse from the beginning but, with Wynwood and *A Time to Kill*, dipped a toe into modern fiction. In the 1990s, Revell had novels by Gilbert Morris and Jane Peart, as well as David Dolan with his end-times novel *The End of the Age* and the Eagle Wings series by Linda Rae Rao. Other fiction authors included Barbara Masci (*Stolen Heritage*), David Biebel (the Rocky Mountain Dossier series), as well as an adaptation of Catherine Marshall's *Christy* for young readers in 1994.

It wasn't until after the purchase by Baker that, under Linda Holland, Revell got serious about increasing the number of fiction titles it published. Jennifer Leep worked with Kathleen Morgan on her historical fiction series Brides of Culdee Creek. Morgan went on to write several more series, such as Heart of the Rockies and These Highland Hills, for Revell, helping to grow the historical fiction genre.

Revell began to acquire new authors who, in turn, started to put Revell on the map, in particular Steven James with his Patrick Bowers novels, Leisha Kelly, and Irene Hannon, who led the publishing house into the genre of romantic suspense.

"Irene wanted to write romantic suspense in addition to her contemporary romances, and we loved what she offered readers," said Leep. "She had an endorsement from Dee Henderson, which gave us a much easier entry into the genre."

Just as Revell was getting traction in fiction, the company bought Bethany House, a publisher with a reputation for high-quality fiction and a large stable of authors. The purchase forced Revell to ask the hard question about whether they should continue to do fiction. The answer was yes.

"The purchase of Bethany was good because it forced us to dig deep, get smarter, and focus on the things we could contribute to the fiction space, such as romantic suspense," said Leep.

Now fiction makes up 50 percent of new titles in a given Revell publishing season, with novels by Ted Dekker, Jane Kirkpatrick, Ann H. Gabhart, Suzanne Woods Fisher, and Lynette Eason drawing readers, and newcomers Susie Finkbeiner and Erin Bartels adding depth to the list.

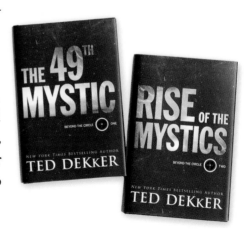

Ann H. Gabhart

© Everlasting Moments Photography by Juanita Jones

Ann H. Gabhart didn't want to be a "Shaker writer." She'd published in the general market for several years with some success before sending her novel *Scent of Lilacs* to Lonnie Hull DuPont at Revell. That novel and two others—*Orchard of Hope* and *Summer of Joy*—were released by Revell starting in 2005. DuPont, during a trip to Tennessee, stopped by Gabhart's Kentucky home to meet the author in person.

"She got lost so was late, so we were able to talk for only twenty minutes. As she was leaving she said she sure wished she had time to visit the Shaker village nearby," said Gabhart. "I threw out that I had written a book about the Shakers many years earlier but general-market publishers didn't want it. I had only a paper copy of it sitting on my shelf."

Gabhart retyped the manuscript into a computer—her computer died twice on the same chapter—and sent it off to Revell. DuPont kept it for about a year until deciding that the visions in the book would be accepted by readers. *The Outsider*, Gabhart's first—and she thought only—Shaker book, came out in 2008.

"Lonnie told me if I'd write two more Shaker books I'd gather more readers, who would then read my other books," said Gabhart. "I've now written eight Shaker books."

Gabhart had a contract for *Angel Sister*, the book of her heart, but it had been tabled for the Shaker novels. DuPont finally took the manuscript for *Angel Sister* with her on an airplane, planning to read it to pass the time. About eighty pages in, her seatmate headed to the restroom. DuPont asked him to throw away the pages she was done with.

"Then she realized she'd given him the pages she hadn't read," said Gabhart. "She decided to get those pages out of the plane bathroom's trash. She waited outside that particular bathroom for a long time, then went in and got her arm down in the wastebasket to pull out those pages. She got back to her seat without anyone thinking she was too crazy. I'm surprised she didn't get arrested."

Angel Sister released in 2011 and is one of Gabhart's most successful novels to date. Gabhart has now published twenty books with Revell.

Heaven, Clean Jokes, and a Blogger

The book *90 Minutes in Heaven: A True Story of Death and Life* by Don Piper and Cecil Murphey changed the landscape for Revell after it released in 2004. Piper's car was hit by a truck, and the paramedics found no pulse and declared him dead. They covered the car with a tarp and waited for the coroner to make the official pronouncement. During the ninety-minute wait, while his body was covered with a tarp in the ruined car, he visited heaven. When a passing minister crawled into the car to pray for him, Piper came back very much alive.

His book was published fifteen years after the events of that fateful day in Texas, and it struck a chord, going on to sell over seven million copies with sales still strong today. Acquiring editor Vicki Crumpton brought the book to the publishing board.

"I had met Don at a writers conference several years before and knew the story. There wasn't any question that I wanted to move forward," said Crumpton. "But not long before the formal proposal arrived, Dwight made the announcement that we weren't pursuing any more personal experience stories. I thought the timing was unfortunate, but I took the project to our publishing committee anyway and they liked it. Fortunately, Dwight made an exception for this project."

That pub board meeting stayed in more than one person's mind.

"I remember, crystal clearly, the meeting when *90 Minutes* was brought up," said Dave Lewis, retired executive vice president of sales and marketing. "I asked Vicki if there were competitive bids, and she said no. I projected ten thousand units sold in the first twelve months."

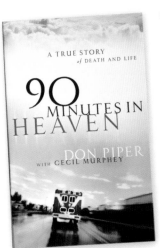

He remembers leaning over to then marketing manager Twila Bennett and saying, "If this book catches on, it has the potential to be the biggest book Revell has ever done."

Jennifer Leep, now executive vice president of trade publishing, said *90 Minutes* elevated the division to a whole new level, from a revenue standpoint. The initial print run of 7,500 was quickly gone and a second printing ordered. Piper was speaking and doing book events in the Houston area, where he lives, and books were selling fast.

In its first year of release, *90 Minutes* sold 33,000 copies; in 2005, it sold 386,000; in 2007, 1.2 million. Revell invested $5,000 in marketing in 2004, then more than $100,000 a year for a couple of years. Piper's rigorous speaking and interview schedule also pushed the sales numbers higher.

"We knew that *90 Minutes* sales would eventually trail off, so our goal was to grow the division enough to maintain those *90 Minutes*

Don Piper

Don Piper didn't write a book to sell millions, to reach tens of millions through speaking and print and radio interviews, or to change the face of Revell publishing. He wrote the book in self-defense.

"I thought that if I put the events of that day down on paper, people would stop asking me about it," said Piper. "I was reliving the accident every day and was asked often how to get through tragedy and loss. I was getting tired of talking about it."

He'd been working on the manuscript for a dozen years when he met Cecil Murphey at a writers conference. Murphey expressed interest in helping Piper write the book, and several months later the process began.

"Cec said the book was either going to be wildly successful or a big bomb," said Piper.

Once the book was completed, Piper attended another writers conference, where he met acquisitions editor Vicki Crumpton. Three other publishers turned him down, but Crumpton and Revell showed interest.

"We got an offer from Revell; it wasn't a big offer, but I didn't care," said Piper. He remembers that, months later, he walked several times through the lobby of First Baptist in Pasadena, Texas, where he was on staff, and saw a package sitting there. He finally opened it, "and I stopped in my tracks. I was holding the book I wrote."

90 Minutes in Heaven came out with little aplomb and little in the way of a marketing budget, but the story began to draw in readers, and Piper was speaking more often.

"I came to Grand Rapids and met with editors and publicity people. I said, 'This is personal. If you go to bat for this book, I will do every interview and go anyplace anytime.' They took me at my word and started booking in obscure, out-of-the-way places. I did them all," he said.

Soon Revell was printing 250,000 books at a time, and Piper continued to talk. Opposite the usual publishing trajectory, Revell released a hardback edition several years after the paperback version.

"A day doesn't pass that I don't receive emails, texts, or phone calls about what the book means to people even fifteen years after it came out and thirty years after the accident," said Piper.

He has traveled the world, from Israel to Scandinavia, Europe to the Far East. He's signed a bootleg copy of an unauthorized Vietnamese translation and a copy that a garbage man found on the top of a trash pile "that he knew was for him." A mother brought a ragged copy she found in her daughter's backpack after she stepped off a bus and was hit and killed. Another mother whose son was killed in Baghdad asked Piper to sign a copy because a nurse had read part of it to the woman's son as he was dying.

"I'm stunned and amazed at how the book has held up, and it started with people like Vicki, a great editor who believed in it," said Piper. "Twila Bennett and Suzy Cross Burden got behind it. I am eternally grateful to Revell and Baker Publishing. I didn't intend to write a bestselling book; I was just trying to help people into heaven and help them have a better trip on the way."

levels," said Leep. "One of the things that makes me most proud of the Revell team is that we've done that. We've exceeded overall sales of our best year with *90 Minutes.*"

Crumpton calls it "truly a work of God. The book isn't explainable apart from God's involvement; we didn't know how much [Piper's] story of recovery would resonate with readers. I've had a couple of colleagues who chose not to pursue the project for their houses say, 'Oops, missed that one.'"

For Lewis, "*90 Minutes* taught us that publishers don't really know anything; books like that take off on their own. We just hang on and shepherd them through the system."

He added, "The brilliant thing Revell editors did was use revenue from *90 Minutes* to acquire new authors who could help keep those levels of sales and sell across a wide range."

Authors such as Mary Beth Chapman and her book *Choosing to SEE: A Journey of Struggle and Hope* (2011) continued Revell's success in the area of personal stories. "Mary Beth's book was a heart book for all of us," said Andrea Doering, now editorial director for Revell. "We wanted to steward that story well, and I've always believed Revell to be the best home for tender stories such as hers."

Holley Gerth, author of *You're Already Amazing* (2012), became one of the first success stories for bloggers turning to books. Her online audience caught the eye of Revell editors because of her knowledge of exactly who her readers were.

Holley Gerth

When Holley Gerth cofounded the (in)courage website back in 2009, there was nothing like it.

© Luke Davis, Main Street Studios

"It's crazy to say it now, but there wasn't an online Christian community for women," said Gerth, who was working for DaySpring Cards. "There wasn't a place for women to gather. DaySpring supported us when we launched it."

Gerth reached out to thirty writers to ask if they'd like to contribute. Only one of those women (Lysa TerKeurst) had published a book. Ann Voskamp and others began to write for (in)courage, with many going on to publish books. Gerth had been blogging since 2008 and had begun to build her audience.

"Jen Leep and I connected in person and we clicked. I loved that while other publishers said they were interested, Jen said that Revell wanted to partner with authors. That relational approach was very different than other companies," said Gerth.

Revell was one of the first to begin publishing bloggers who had built an audience.

"People used to say that blogging wasn't real writing, but blogging helps an author build a body of work that connects with community," said Gerth. "I think it helped for Revell to know that I was already in that space, creating content, and deeply invested in the hearts of women."

Gerth's next book, about introverts, comes out in the fall of 2020. She continues to blog and is still a regular contributor to (in)courage.

"I love it that Revell tends to see changes as opportunities instead of roadblocks," she said.

"I met Holley in 2010," said Leep. "Her content was great, she's a gifted writer, and she knew clearly who her reader was. As we began looking at bloggers, we realized they weren't that different from speakers in that they're still communicators. And Holley really listened to her audience."

Revell has published ten books by Gerth—five trade books and five devotionals—with sales totaling into the millions.

Another Revell milestone was the Laugh-Out-Loud Jokes for Kids series by Rob Elliott. Rob Teigen—Elliott's real name—had worked for Harvest House, which had a series of popular joke books that he helped sell. When he came to Revell as a special market sales rep, he suggested a similar book or books to Lonnie Hull DuPont. She thought this was a fine idea and said he could write it. Teigen, with help from his wife and three daughters, decided to give it a try.

Laugh-Out-Loud Jokes for Kids released in 2010, with sales of 15,000 that year. Sales increased steadily to a high of 613,000 in 2015. It still sells 200,000 to 250,000 a year and has been a *USA TODAY* and *Wall Street Journal* bestseller. It was number one on Amazon's Top 100 Books list for three consecutive years during the holiday season, and one of Amazon's Top 20 bestselling children's books of all time.

Soon after came *Knock-Knock Jokes for Kids* (2013), *More Laugh-Out-Loud Jokes for Kids* (2014), *Laugh-Out-Loud Animal Jokes for Kids* (2014), and various compilations of these four books. The brand as a whole has sold 3.5 million copies.

Celebrating 150 Years

Revell has kept its focus on readers through 150 years of publishing. Beginning with Sunday school papers at the request of Fleming

Rob (Elliott) Teigen

Rob Teigen took a job in special market sales at Baker Publishing Group. Before he knew it, he was cracking jokes with his family and writing them down for a joke book.

"When I suggested a joke book to Lonnie, she said I should write it. When the proposed book was presented to Dave Lewis, he said, 'But he's not even that funny,'" said Teigen. "I got the last laugh on that one."

"We started with my family around the dinner table. My kids would bring jokes they heard at school, and we'd tweak them and make them funnier," said Teigen, who lives in West Michigan. "We did a lot of play on words, but we came up with a lot of them on our own."

What started as a bit of a lark has become much more. Teigen hears often from parents and grandparents about the joy and laughter that come with the jokes.

"Parents say it's helped their kids enjoy reading and build confidence in their reading. One mom said it was the first book her daughter with dyslexia read cover to cover," said Teigen. "She started a nonprofit for kids with dyslexia and bought a case of the joke books."

Teigen recently heard about a hospital that purchased a bunch to hand out to hospitalized kids. "An email from the hospital said, 'If you could hear the laughter we hear.'

"You think it's a silly little joke book compared to the amazing books Revell has put out over the years, but it's had a huge impact," he said. "It's so rewarding on so many levels I never thought possible."

His favorite joke? What do you get when you throw a pig in the bushes? A hedgehog.

"I realize I have a lot of parents who hate me. They tell me that their kids bring the book in the car, and after a hundred jokes, they want to find me and hurt me," he said, laughing.

Teigen recently left his sales job and began writing full time with his wife, Joanna. They have written for Christian Art Gifts and other publishers. Their most recent books, *Powerful Prayers for Your Daughter* and *Powerful Prayers for Your Son* (both 2019) are with Revell.

Revell's famous brother-in-law, moving into theological titles and sermon compilations, and on to trade titles and fiction, Revell has always turned its heart to the readers.

What do readers want? What do readers need? Who speaks best to those readers? These are questions asked daily at Revell.

"The more we think about what the reader is looking for, the better the bottom line," said Leep.

Personal growth and practical help continue to be the hallmark of the house. "We focus much of our publishing on practical hope and help—ideas and concepts readers can carry with them throughout their day," said editorial director Andrea Doering.

Books released in 2019 and 2020 include *The Next Right Thing: A Simple, Soulful Practice for Making Life Decisions* by Emily P. Freeman and *Saints: Becoming More Than "Christians"* by Addison D. Bevere.

Long-popular Revell authors continue to write and sell: a new edition of *The Intimate Connection: Secrets to a Lifelong Romance* by

Dr. Kevin Leman; *Character Carved in Stone: The 12 Core Virtues of West Point That Build Leaders and Produce Success* by Pat Williams and Jim Denney; a repackaged edition of *Wired That Way Personality Profile* by Marita and Florence Littauer; and a repackaged edition of *The Journals of Jim Elliot*, edited by Elisabeth Elliot.

Fiction continues as a mainstay of the Revell line, with well-known authors continuing to publish and new voices, such as Tari Faris, James R. Hannibal, Natalie Walters, Shawn Smucker, and Bethany Turner, being nurtured as well.

The author remains just as important, however. "Our job is to steward these authors' stories. We've learned by experience to understand the real person behind the story," said Leep. "He or she might be talking about what happened, but it's still happening for them. The story is living and present and ongoing. Our role is to be mindful, to care for the author, to take time to understand and ask about how they're doing in the process."

There have been tough years thanks to hard economic times, leadership changes, the occasional flop that costs the company

c. 1906–1924

1925–1947

1948–1962

money. There have also been good times as bestsellers take off, the company stabilizes, and the Revell family grows together.

"Revell is part of the heart of Baker Publishing Group," said president Dwight Baker. "We were honored to purchase it and are honored to help in its success. My father, Richard Baker, was smart to buy it; my grandfather, Herman Baker, would have loved to be part of it. I pray that we can continue to help uphold the long legacy of Revell."

1962–1977   1979–1992   1992–present